BROWNUP

AND OTHER POEMS

BY RON WELBURN

The Greenfield Review Press
Greenfield Center, N.Y. 12833

Greenfield Review Chapbook No. 32

ISBN-0-912678-32-1

© Copyright 1977 Ron Welburn

Cover Photo by Mary Ann Lynch

Design by Doug Bradway

Some of these poems originally appeared in *Bim, Black World, The Black Voice* (Syracuse University). Acknowledgement is due their editors for permission to reprint.
The Ash Tree, Black History Museum Umum Newsletter, YWCA, Mundus Artium, Giant Talk.

Publication of this book has been made possible, in part, by a Small Press Grant from the New York State Council on the Arts.

For my grandmother, Laura

Contents

HARLEQUINFUSIONS

I

PERCUSSIONS

NEW MORNING PRAYER

dance
it is new light
in our space of expression
our past is darker
and warm and unashamed

dance
sing while you
move your feet the ways
blood show you how to
move your hands
run down a tale a myth
a folk science rapsodied
endowed by heaven

dance
and hope
and be not afraid
of being
happiness so
sing and
dance rap out
a story
clap hands ring memories
throw the heads back to future

dance
it is new light
new prayers
if it is
new guinea sounds
and figi hair
pharoah horns filled
with piano waters
our Creator did it then when

he made this earth and sky
and sea
and hell
go ahead

dance.

Black World, July 1973.

PIANO

piano
such a sweet way
and tell me a story
cover me a song or
bathe me in images of how you feel
God or lesser
ranks of men

downhome for this one
not like organ sound or
piano-with-buttons
but now high nepalian ceremony
to another
kilaminjaro peak above clouds
or strain of blues
fertile shadows dancing
red in the mind

is drum is piano
tell a story
coded soft or full
as expression parts
or images
and voices with bright
or blue faces

o faces
kiss me a story.

EXEMPLARS

ants
are
foot soldiers
invaders
of our privacy
from beneath walls
which be their own
privacy
of motives and
homing

workers
or
fighters
they are not quite
"revolutionaries"
but carry off
their casualties
crushed by our
weight

ants
are
a peculiar society
a sophisticated working order
a bit more
outtasight
than our own
or
what we'd like it to be.

JUAN DE PAREJA*

juan de pareja   today
is the most expensive nigger
in the world
in the whole wide world

is guarded closer than joe frazier
or ali

      so close perhaps
his brothers can't get to him
shake his stalwart hand or
slap him five

too close perhaps
to his buyers
will have him watched keenly
the way of day hawkers and owl nights
while he rests there
outlined against an opaque wall
decked in thick rich vines
and
a superb afro
looking still as though his first patrons

"expected it to speak"

like malcolm even.

12 May 1971

*Juan de Pareja was a mulatto servant to the 17th-century
Spanish painter Diego Velasquez. He sat for a portrait which
eventually became the most expensive painting in the world.
The painting was so lifelike some observers said "we expected it
to speak."

MORE THAN SONGS CAN TELL

rain afterthoughts
mystic aeolian animals
scurry over drum be it meadow
and meadowlark's sweet
victory song

the lyric
the rhythm of
this affection
more than songs can tell

ray charles, johnny hartman
the dells, and smokey miracles
more than songs

compassion if complete enough
and full cup spilling
over out of magic of words
in blue green yellow songs
breast of that meadowlark
bursting with lyric
my nana memorized
and could tell me
when he was there afield unseen
speaking the tongue
more than his song can tell.

PRETENSES

some days be
dog days
scar tissue thinner
on our backs
spite of temper
atures
cold or heated

we would go around here
arrogant defiant
mad in pride
and dance to any music
that dialates us its pupils

high-fly   then
run amok   look
away looking at each other high
and standing there
wasted and weak

as griffons come out of the woodwork.

UNINTENTIONALLY

sensitive words
or coldness turns back
dead leaves

gags forgotten phlegm
to mix with quiet words
careful
and yet our paths
singularly into awkward
gothic caves
least we then dare go
any further

cat look on
our faces and that ugly
memorial of dancing
to the choked voice
of a broken drum.

Black History Museum Umum Newlsetter
July-Aug., 1973

DAY LIGHTNING AND RAIN

day lightning and rain
with the sun out already
devil knockin fool out he wife
who done come up this way
daytime to plant her harvest of death
brothers runnin in e rain
to whatcha'callum's
for shelter
but not this older head
with the pint a crow in his pocket
swaggerin like this still
improvising on sun an lightning
and beating time
to that static radio drum.

TOP OF THE WORLD

the alley is a refuge
a promised land
where live all gods divine
image

yes still these
women with their heads out of
second-story windows
and their toothpaste
left for sparrows to catch

a bootlegger's room
as a kind of red sea opening up
from the alley and leading back
to it wherever it is you go
shapes objects pursue you
times you never leave
times you go and never reach heaven
you end up wasted on the trolley
out in foreign country
where white folks look strange at you

to sober up
you can return to the bean cans
hoisted above the refuse
that children make.

this is the top of the world.

you can be annointed next morning
when they open the windows again
the sparrows—
trying to catch it
hanging from their long faces.

despite the sign of the soil
the sweeping arms length of mountains
the hollowing of valleys
there are no stones in my mouth
anymore
or charred forests dead weight
on my shoulders

songs are these what
I know of earth
and venus bright neighbor of mornings
or evenings love can be
vespers for the life in close warmth
of nights and
following day

morning prayers a diversity of heritage
wherewe are coming from

indigenous musics for the dance
and the meditations resolve this
so our lives burn into each other
like rain into august rivers
day into the sounds of drumming

we reach out for our Creator
and touch our blood spinning
yoruba and swiss ashanti and scotch
madras lenape bodies
of masters chained to their slaves
and comforters spawning us thus
here headed back
upstream to mountain
place of our beginning
place of our rest
peace of tranquility our memoirs.

The Ash Tree No. 3
November, 1973

SPILLINGS

passing the teenaged
sisters bearing
new warriors
who
have tried suckling
at too young breasts
sorrow suckles
within the bellies
of the Nation
some bellies you
would deny me this:

a standard
rightfully so
but
the seeds
of us
go

right on

into nights
and
make boredom
heavy with child.

we must bring these progeny
to restful slumber
with muted valved horns
and wake them
invincible
with whispers of worth.

TIRED TRADE
for Andrew Hill

we ought to be
long exhausted
bellies full
of playing this masque
our lives and futures stretched
handled like merchandise
in a tired trade
we open doors violently
and get squeezed through
from an eye-dropper
are show-stoppers
on elaborate decor
of new auction blocks
programmed by TV
and deprivation
that makes petty thievery
a skill for us
and waste
a sacrament of absolution.

TOWN AND COUNTRY

a
working mother
                    soon
                            leaves
                        her
            shuttled
son
out
        where
                dew
                        rises home
                        in her heart
        where
                vultures
spin
        webs
                in the
                        window skies
out
        where
                he
                        can pick strawberries

and
    crush
        new
           walnuts
even kill large cellar rats
a
mother
      may
         soon
           leave

her son
      with
         the
           trees he loves
green
but
    related
       to
         some
       prior
    strange
fruit.

sons who missed being
their father's sons
and almost the memory
of mothers
a few short paces
uncertain from childbirth
are the experiences
forgotten in the slow white rain
of toothpaste from the alley windows
sometime imperceptibly in the morning
fish bone along the soup can way

laughter songs return to touch
across the street, a haverford avenue,
they built snowmen in januaries
a monument to insurance men
and the secret nights whispered
by summer rains
at les's store they traded in their pennies
for sweets: vision:
the puerto rican children or the filipinos
the little girl next door on the stoop
where a man in a cap drunk
threatened to cut a child's throat
a man with one leg watched
then hungrily paced the floor in his way
curious to the child

what kind of impressions are made
in these years of shitting in alleys
seeing how little girls went to the bathroom
or silently
no consciousness of
some father there to blame them.

TAKE YOUR FISH WITH YOU

faith lost or
bitten
clings to its memory
and
clings faster to its abuse

the same
when the crab or lizard
turns on you and leaves
a mark
if you wring your whole arm
to
fling it miles away.

PATRONS

to be in a place one
whole year and have no idea
None!
this bitter feeling than desert venture
blackeness in snowe countrye
guyless in eyela
sacrifice is good but no—
your tongue when you are called
upon to give directions—
how to get out of it from here—
paranoid shortman
temper sways its shield
fratricide looms distant painted
horizon wall leaning next to you

those who are armed with emotion
plot in the deliberate fervor of patrons
on record who said they listened to
monk at the blackhawk or
dolphy at the five spot
fullnoise their inquisitions
a gesture of professional pariahs
come or been this way

(when you don't know what you want to do
you try doing five six things at once
and if you live through the summer
wake up exhausted discovering you
can only do one of those very well
and perhaps another nearly so
and the rest you either must hand down
to childhood or walk away from them

or put them in a portfolio of spoiled records)
take it to your inquisitors
and throw it lovingly at their faces.

PERCUSSIONS

we have these drums
you know stretched
over the balafon earth
australia to haiti
bahia to harlem
kimberly to cairo
quick fingers slapping
under reeds flutes or horns
pharoah's prayers vibrate
the diaphrammed world
from the eye of the universe
singing that is strange souls
nothing you or I heard from
guinea these new guinea melodies
this must be the way we first
raised our voices in celebration
this is the way our ancestors
hearts must have beat tight in breasts
this is the way ti-roro and patato
learned the immense depth of life itself
we speak our arms wrists palms and fingertips
gone beyond wearisome aching
we have this will of expression
you know drums and kinds of naked pianos
and horns beat on
brightly you know for song.

Black World, Sept. 1972
Giant Talk, (Random House)

PROCEPTION

```
W                    E
   r
a      a        a            aLLLLLL
ina
s  p  a  C I o u s
R     o        o      M
u
n    abl        e
to              ssssseeeeeeeeeeeeeeeeeeeee
our             sellllllvvvveessssssssss
THINK
our
sssssellllvvvvessssssss
a     b
      s    urd
t          urd
      s
```

LOOKING FOR THIRD WORLDS

service to the lips
of the third world
whatever you think it is
on a reservation in new mexico
or new yorkstate
el barrio or the othernamed ghetto
the mind outside of you
puts chinatown in the
affluent bag of japanese honeys
from phoenix whose fathers
were wire-meshed in countenance
you don't have to look very far
brothers not even to
the lips of fanonfidelomao
bandung conferees
ride the subways everyday
if you desperate enough
you might even rob one
and kill another for no
apparent reason no particular joke
to hell with africa asia latino
just look at yourself closelike
and turn up the music.

Black World
September 1972

MAZES HAZES

for John S. Walker (Tarik Abdul)

there are days
when mazes hazes
make you a whole new sky
or nightime horizon
early or late lips of the world
and ellipsis swings out of your mouth
call it night   or day
call it   off ruby minor night
good ruby love in the night
sky with a low new moon
the palette of stars sucks
you through it and you will
go gladly or be swallowed
into the belly of the universe.

PISCES DAYS
for Charlie Fuller

fridays
you get a fish
eye view
of the blackworld
an oceanic consciousness
afro figi
whose ass was kicked
by our brothers
sediment collects in our mouths
and ears
meat hangs slowly
from the rim
looking out of this lens
our gills suck up stagnant water
we are long-time bottom feeders
when there is no light
who on earth or sea needs eyes?

The Ash Tree, No. 2
August, 1973

II

DUSK BE OUR SABBATH

DAY ELEVEN

I listen to singalong
with days I felt
longtime for you could be
found here
warm flesh in
the City or northern town days
I am in pennsyltucky
this day tension
of money scratching
dogs of flea jungles
and I will never adjust to water
am desertman to seas though fisher
of lakesides only
drinkin a li'l rum n water
this day this one down
to anothergone
I share with you
my arrogance
and blood so.

OUT ON A LIMB

day seven
curving eleven
I am near out on a limb
guiseppi logan
piano in my head
at night I'm tossing
with your brown ankles
whirling through my sleep
so it is
from us
togethering
when longing will
burst into stars and
dusk
shall be our sabbath.

Black History Museum Newsletter.
July-Aug 1973

BAY BROWN WINDOW

your settling at the window
a bay apparatus with lips on the sea
take in that breathsweeping scape of
blue green while it cajols roars
around the dark of your face

you settled in the crook of my arm
forcing sunset's rays bend into
christ church a kind of monument
that window was you image of stillness
in bolder relief honeybrown against
already wood   you and the solemn
earthy textures of nature.

pub. in BIM, July-Dec, 1972

IN BIMSHIRE TIME

1

sun island of no
particular time no
schedule will make
the bus run or the rain
regular in its season

the sun will be there to
morrow we wake or not and
the long day and the worker
will exchange blows of tedious
patience

the long battle
persistent as night frogs singing
romance

and who will come up
this dusk as winner?

2

these kin of distance beating the drum
of the hot afternoon
these rays of the gods beating flesh
of toil and rhythm
Bajun holds his back straight
though time
and the sun
on his back
are obvious in the legended scourge
in his feet

sun may be riddle of patience
as well as the master drummer
who will beat us all until
the bus is filled and it
is time to

move out from bridgetown
day effort
always revolves on this

the stranger black or the canadian can
not rely on this thing riddle called time
you want to move on
and do as surely as
the persistence of dawn over coconut trees
someone will bring you along

and the paler tourists
though not the clear-skinned brothers
may buy up your shores
for your prosperity
may manage you
food and money centers

what life does to you like jacob
wrestling with it
to find solace in the coral of seas or
the motion of the mind and spirits elves
from colonial cane-cutting to
pushing a pen
or the wanting to be
apple-picking in canada.

3
this is nothing idyllic
and then is
from the confusion of stateside
and continent
the motorcar as a hazardous gesture

all over the latin world
is so soon
in the impulse of donkey wake

30

but read still on
at bus stations
and keep the folks be frugal
save that honesty and island home
save that proud beauty of Bimshire
though you will parry for it
with the thrusting sun.

LATIN MOON

life is latinful
moon near equator night
the face of a flying fish
rise and go back and forth
into americas

flock of herons mostly bittern
though do the mating dance
with the neck and timbales
in the wingbeat

the flight pattern translated
from the spanish
from creole
from a patios the king's english

latin moon goes swift
to heat
and the nights fleet through our
passions

day gallops through the antilles
like a gaucho run from the pampas
pursuing an evasive song.

TOBAGO DAWN

a tobago pastoral
at dawn
      looms outside belief
so poets have raised lyrics
to the coconut trees and the bays

we act out crusoe
or more his friday servant
here on the literate imagination
brought here dawns
in dutch and latin ships

we live in a wilderness barren
of roads and peopled with beauty
if we are all closer to nature feel
its first tremoring to westworld's advance
wires of speaking Rediffusion
      pollute this morning of
      my view though
how else
might we have seen this dawn

we would be caught up in
the sweet smells of groves and
ponder the golf course nearby
as visitors to this hidden rock
eastward nearing some anniversary
      of freedom
westwardly awaiting
      its spoilage.

OFTENER RAINS

the
often
er rains

bring
us

       blessings
       fertile
       earth

you are

       soon as we
       vowed
       &
       danced
       in

bajun
august
and
tobago

water prayed

          to
          can
          purify

our
sacramented
selves
at an alter

          rains
          oftener
          than
          your
          father's

tears
moistening
the space

        the
        shadow of

our
nestled
sleep.

SAVAGES TREES

ashanti and lenape
seems
do their dances
modified
by the form of
lips and noses

africa
to island west
mainland soul
and
warrior rituals

so part of me is mocassin trail
across my face and in
my eyes fire like vengence

though africaine
be my spirit self

whatever we be scotch
of name turned good blessing
from the phoenix of lyrics
I can speak no language
other than song or chant
heart is my rhythm

is my continuous throbbing drum.

THE SKIN OF MANY DRUMS

love is like
a triplet of mountains
rhythmblessed of bosom full
with sunshine and soft

brown enough to warm up
an ocean's tonguing
her flanks

love is like cubano bop
a rhumba walking
through these newyorkstatestreets
and spanish gesticulations

love is an island
naive in the sun and
naive in the churning flesh
like the skins of many drums.

Mundus Artium
VIII, No. 1, 1975

BROWNUP

your brown
heat in white december
face in the sky air of song
is your laughter of rain

long waiting and a walk about
be brown in the heat of my name

in this wintering
you provoke praisesong
and warrior rejoicing

my heart that drum
once beating away wishes
sentiment echoes through me now
shoulder to toes
covered brown your eyes heated.

III

HARLEQUINFUSIONS

THE YOUNG BLACK WRITERS

for Bill Welburn, Charles Harpe,
Charyn Sutton, Alice Foster
Tony Bennia, Jube Shiver,
Stephanie Hamilton

one
test
of
young
writers'
endurance

is
that
they
will
SURVIVE

their earliest
immature
efforts

their earliest
memories

their
strongest
poverty
of
images
and
rhythm.

BURGEST AT TUCUMCARI
(for David R. B.)

had breakfast there two
mornings   holiday
in twenty-fourth winter I crossed
the flatlands between eastern skies

"this land aint got nuthin"
they will tell you
where live the pronghorn
venturing out to highways
and the coyote calling in
the nahuatl tongue
south and east into comanche places
what are we here our faces dark
as mesa from the air
our limbs sinewy as shadow
mountains we leave and our fates
gone to amarillo bleakness
but leave cities for this heart
land
ever think about what if could
grow here or who could live?

we had all migrated here in our dreams
of a hundred years   singleton to delany
we had found the way back to lizard
trail   you leave one town or path
and do not see another
what brothers here before you or I
passing through or trekked into
the western hills
are they gone or do they dwell
in antelopes and the spirit of rocks?

at tucumcari there is coffee and muses of
space   land   while there I wondered
why we had all run to cities.

LED FROM TEMPTATIONS

days wake up evil
to you off n on
to believe in music
                more than womenmen
or the belief
projected on musicians
as lesser kind of gods
                soothes
the mad
conscious level

it's good to know when
days wake up evil
this
is where you can end up.

DALI-ING

I might be a softer voice
now but hard
hammer eyes scrape your silent repose
fire eyes narrow
myself into the dali world

    "soft construction
       with boiled beans"

a motif within premonition
here with you now
head and calf-piece
mixed with peppers in a bean pie
europa's cauldrons here can adapt

though what I see
hides in the fires of its own mouth
deceipt again
is suckling child to madness
come round our way bopping
in the sunrise rhythm of summer

so I am here
muting the tenored terror's heart
am eater of slow flame and
can temper the quick of these winters
long autumn song dances along deadened streets
newsprint in grass reading
the signs of illness in the skies
where my echo
leaps arms akimbo to ellipsis
to prayer
walking in distress
to another outer world.

Mundus Artium
VIII, No. 1, 1975

POSTURES

listen
to the strength
of long singing
coming out of black faces

saxophones or
fingers rapid
alternate haze
the sun
and rain
the tears and smiles
of our yearning
we bear our heads
bent from upright
our stooped shoulders
heavy with lyrics
natural with
rhythm
that do be
somehow
looking up.

Black World, July 1973.

SUNDRAMA

sun go down
fingered by trees

buildings hanging
touch the ground

light wood in shadow
over us and in our
heads of course all
ways of questions

tulips to the west
rose petal lawn all
ways of foliage from
when we walked where
leaves gesture
in ceremony
prior to the time of
those their structures

precariously monolithic
relics of a stone age
after the sun when
caressed by trees sits
indolent a cookie

whimsically we might
steal it if not it were
pasted there mocking
our losses of heart or food
depravity and affluence

radiating the drama
given our color changes.

BRAKE'S SAKE
for Monk

from 't'
to 'z'
or around again to
sake of the brake
need be given us
once in a strange while
you wait for cane
on long summers
come in
from stormy moons
dancing there aint
no music
before
sway around the piano
in italian suede wheels
ring at you nose
from the fist
tenor you have to lean
a new tune loon
cry in swamps of cities
chief new york is an island
sinking fast
Lord give us uptown please
a break!

LAND OF THE BLIND

what do we
look
like here
takin the time
helpin a blind
man through traffic
or he be leadin us
our brothers in trucks
or sisters on lawns sandaled
look at me say
if they senses can cut
the absurdity of it
if not
a blind man
my spectators
and then
Me
with one eye.

ATTICA

picked up where
dachau left its mark
this civilization
brothers enguarded have their
bodies luxury of stews
their meat savoring palettes
of the wealthy
and the armed

so they are closing down internment camps
so we all abide within circles of fire
oftener quick
draw lightning punctures our desperation
mood of men and machines
alive it is a waste who
are mated poverty and pain
we are enough within walls
to be leaders of such burials
stillgone unnoticed in the news
these wastes sanctified in sabbaths

if there is no light or bulb
in the heart building the wall
if there is no future
when you live scurvied in filth allowed
take the lessons most dear
manifest the survival urge
fittest though downed.

HOPES ARE FULL OF BLISTERS

hopes of night places
and faces are full of blisters
we sweatin out dis hyere liberation
thing in the evening yard
mowing another's lawn
picked cotton all day and
sing songs nighttime
abrasive clods flying
in the air in the wind those
latins we think
happier than we
are in their rhythms and shoes
designed for thin ankles
life is stranger than science
and sometimes fiction
life is learning and sometimes
even stronger than
forgotten drums our ancestral voices
calling
calling
telling and
calling
are starting to get
blisters
from our hands.

SYRACUSE IN HARLEQUIN-FUSION
for Al & Willie

when would sun
shine here
         often as
the seldom arrogance of warm day
against snow
           on we
here dark and scattered leaves
blend only the summer scene
thought here a harlequin design
crude hues in a cabinet of the mind
and thought anathema to the starched
desert of these years

how long?   that evening . . . . ?
not even trains run
how long?   not whistle hooting blues
disturbed of spirit and fingers
arms hearts amputated with itching
from the middle later passage

trek north followed by san juan
trek following tomahawk trail underbrush gone
long as harlequinfusion
run around   no tracks make you
run around   white man we say make you
run around   harlequinfusion we make you
run around   deny it

("the world is a jug"
of dirty water we in its sinking
barrel
crabs   you know the rest . . . .)
we will deny   you
will deny

repetition without skill is redundancy
sonny rollins after a retirement
always sounds better more musical than
our vainer attempts at song and lyric
we are become words backwards
feigning african sound we
can neither spell nor articulate
clear as robinsong or jay's
harsh squaking in the dead trees

masters of long dawn's deception
makes us masters of our own
destruction in the twilight of their world
who are we but sheep   or some
masquarading jesus trick at supper
or wanting crosses to bear or what we think
he was   risen
was renaissance man
we still in and deeperdoubt to the tired trade
of any one's effort
serious to the wolves of crises

how long   not train
no more   sunlight rides about
in wasted vehicles or curb walked or stood on
in the midafter noonday harvesting
manner of all despair
how long?
this place of another harlem numbered
as pennies frequent from the mint
how long?
evenin train in red black green
steam of the moon   how long?
in harlequinfusion   run run runaround
standin
missed the train again
at the station.

MORNING PRAYERS

coltrane's music and pharoah
in tandem
make us believe
in a God
a Creator whose ears are so big
he charts our decisions
and scatters us like ants
swept by winds

do we a cross to bear
or crescents carrying our
spawned to broken responsibility?

record waxes they made
should now be tallow
prayerbooks

we ought to bend
to these scriptures
without smoke
once each day:
in the morning early.

SANDY, NO. 2

speak softly
of   the   sun   going   down

e
l
s
e

the
l   i   z   a   r   d   s
hear
you

YOU HAVE IN MY LIFE

you have in my life
yours
as some whistling newborn

as weight tests my stance
draws out
the measure of faith

your eyes big beckon brown
your hips thighs relax
your lips moist part dry
my own
mouth opens
but it will not speak.

FRIENDS

ghosts
somehow
think about us
remember to stop by
to see us
to chat with us in
the living room or the kitchen
wake us from slumber
with their restless walking
through nostalgia
if we are kind enough
if we leave them fruit
or mist of incense
they
will protect us
and guard our homes
when we're away.

WREN

be
a lazy afternoon

for me
be

a dove or a wren
be

a wren

have courage.

SETTING FOR A LATER PRAYER

one
sureday
we'll
pass through
the desert

kneel
in front of
rocky
alters

lord
will hear us
thank
him
for our
many
blessings

and
music
will come from
an organ-pipe

a kind of cactus
that is.